Instant Oracle BPM for Financial Services How-to

Discover how to leverage BPM in the financial sector

B. M. Madhusudhan Rao

BIRMINGHAM - MUMBAI

Instant Oracle BPM for Financial Services How-to

First published: April 2013

Production Reference: 1180413

Published by Packt Publishing Ltd.
Livery Place
35 Livery Street
Birmingham B3 2PB, UK.

ISBN 978-1-78217-014-3

www.packtpub.com

Credits

Author
B. M. Madhusudhan Rao

Reviewer
Birender Singh

Acquisition Editor
Erol Staveley

Commissioning Editor
Ameya Sawant

Technical Editor
Manmeet Singh

Project Coordinator
Sneha Modi

Proofreader
Dirk Manuel

Production Coordinator
Prachali Bhiwandkar

Cover Work
Prachali Bhiwandkar

Cover Image
Nilesh Mohite

Foreword

Oracle's BPM Suite is a part of Oracle's Fusion Middleware (FMW) family of products. Oracle has been working on BPM technologies for many years, and has integrated various technologies from multiple acquisitions and its core FMW products into the current release of Oracle BPM Suite PS6 (11.1.1.7).

Oracle's BPM Suite is well-suited to work in the Financial Services Industry due to the time-sensitive nature of this business. Oracle's BPM Suite can be used to automate and monitor many common business processes, in order to increase the end customer's satisfaction leading to increased overall profitability.

This book contains a series of examples, highlighting how Oracle's BPM technology can be applied to some very common and recognizable business processes in the financial services industry. This is a great tool for someone in the financial services industry to use to become more familiar with Oracle's BPM offering.

Madhusudhan Rao has worked at Oracle for over five years, supporting customers in a variety of industries, including financial services. Prior to joining Oracle, Madhu worked at HCL Technologies. Madhu works from Oracle's offices in Bangalore, India and supports Oracle's North American customers. He has extensive experience with Oracle's BPM Suite, as well as Oracle's overall FMW Suite. He is an active blogger and participates in various online forums and communities.

Jack Kingsley
Senior Sales Consulting Director
North America Technology Organization India and Apps/Tech Teams
Oracle Corporation.

About the Author

B. M. Madhusudhan Rao, alias name James Smith (Author of James Smith's Technology Blogs), has more than 15 years of experience in the enterprise software industry. He has been a TOGAF 9 Enterprise Architecture certified solution specialist at Oracle's North America Technology Organization for more than 5 years. He works primarily around Service Oriented Architecture, Business Process Management, Webcenter Portal, Webcenter Content, and Enterprise Architecture Practice. He is a part of the Tech-Sales team that showcases various customer proof of concepts and demonstrations to meet the customers' business challenges and requirements.

Before joining Oracle, Madhu was a Technical Manager at HCL Technologies in India. He is known as James for his blog *James Smith's Java and Oracle Blogs*, which is very popular among techies. Last year, in 2012, his blog `jamessmith73.wordpress.com` had over 74,000, hits making it one of the top technology blogs.

Madhu lives in Bangalore,India with his parents, wife, and little daughter Aishwarya Rao, and loves nature photography.

I would like to thank my management team, Jack Kingsley, Oracle North America Technology Sales Consulting Senior Director, for his support without which writing this book would have not been possible. I would also like to thank Senior Vice President Michael Weingartner from Integration Product Management and Senior Vice President Anthony Fernicola from the North America Sales Organization. I would also like to thank my Manager Sudershan Singh, Sales Consulting Manager for the SOA BPM Webcenter Team at North America Technology Sales Organization for his help and support while writing this book.

About the Reviewer

Birender Singh has 12 years of IT industry experience, which includes 4 years of Sales Consulting. He has significant experience in development, support, consulting, and pre-sales.

He is based out of Bangalore, India, focusing on Service Oriented Architecture (SOA), Business Process Management (BPM), and WebCenter Pillar. He also has good integration knowledge of Oracle Applications such as E-Business Suite R11i and R12, and has worked on various opportunities for building integrations.

www.PacktPub.com

Support files, eBooks, discount offers and more

You might want to visit www.PacktPub.com for support files and downloads related to your book.

Did you know that Packt offers eBook versions of every book published, with PDF and ePub files available? You can upgrade to the eBook version at www.PacktPub.com and as a print book customer, you are entitled to a discount on the eBook copy. Get in touch with us at service@packtpub.com for more details.

At www.PacktPub.com, you can also read a collection of free technical articles, sign up for a range of free newsletters and receive exclusive discounts and offers on Packt books and eBooks.

http://PacktLib.PacktPub.com

Do you need instant solutions to your IT questions? PacktLib is Packt's online digital book library. Here, you can access, read and search across Packt's entire library of books.

Why Subscribe?

- ► Fully searchable across every book published by Packt
- ► Copy and paste, print and bookmark content
- ► On demand and accessible via web browser

Free Access for Packt account holders

If you have an account with Packt at www.PacktPub.com, you can use this to access PacktLib today and view nine entirely free books. Simply use your login credentials for immediate access.

Instant Updates on New Packt Books

Get notified! Find out when new books are published by following @PacktEnterprise on Twitter, or the *Packt Enterprise* Facebook page.

Table of Contents

Preface

Enterprise Organizations are increasingly adopting Oracle Business Process Management (BPM) to increase their organizational efficiency and excellence. As per industry analyst reports, such as those from Gartner and Forrester, BPM has been at the top of the senior management focus list for the last four to five years, and BPM spending has been at a multi-billion dollar level. BPM's ability to streamline the business process and integrate with business partners has been a key focus area both from an IT and business point of view. BPM's out-of-the-box capabilities with respect to human workflow, notifications, simulations, integration with various applications through adapters and document management systems had been a key factor both from a Solution Architecture and Development view of a Business process.

BPM is built on Oracle's SOA (Service Oriented Architecture) Suite infrastructure. BPM Suite 11g provides enhanced support for application integration services, business events, Web 2.0, E2.0, and high scalability. BPM has sufficient easy-to-use features to make it also suitable for small to complex enterprise projects.

This book covers various aspects of BPM from a financial services point of view, and looks at how BPM can help in various organizational roles such as Process Administrator, Process Analyst, Process Owner, and Process Participants. Each of the recipes cover a how-to-do activity. We start with setting up the development environment to integrate with a business partner and end at a complete enterprise portal, which helps in achieving an organization's goals and customer satisfaction.

What this book covers

Setting up the development environment (Simple), discusses some of the key challenges faced in the financial services industry such as banks, mortgage firms, insurance companies, stock brokerage firms, and so on. We will also be setting hands on a development environment and configuring Oracle BPM, Webcenter Portal, and Webcenter Content to work together.

Modeling a home loan business process (Intermediate), is seen more from a process analyst's perspective that comprises of modeling the business process, setting up business rules to determine Platinum/Gold or non-eligible customers for a home loan. These business rules are editable by the process analyst at a later point in time as and when business requirements change.

Implementing a home loan business process (Advanced), shows how a process developer would implement some of the core logic to calculate the EMI amount for the requested loan amount for a given period of time at a rate of interest decided by the business analyst. There are different EMI options—fixed and variable EMI—that customers can choose from. The auto-generated IDs can be used across the loan application process up to loan fulfillment.

Deploying and testing a process workflow (Advanced), takes a closer look at the home loan process. It covers workflow approvals from one stage to another based on the organization's hierarchy. We will also discuss some of the core BPMN modeling techniques and service re-usability across the process, some of the best practices, deployment and process testing.

Administering processes (Advanced), discusses process escalation, setting process deadlines, document management capabilities, process simulation, and cost and time analysis that helps the process owner take some of the key business decisions in an overall business process.

Changing a business process by the process analyst (Advanced), covers process change management, and the process audit trail in detail, it also demonstrates using the process composer to edit and change the business rules and the process flow as per the changes in the business requirement.

Creating business reports for process owners (Intermediate), covers some of the key real-time reporting requirements of the business process owners. This recipe covers the business activity monitoring application to track the real-time process data in BAM dashboard and helps the process owner in making some of the key decisions with respect to the business.

Participating in a business process (Intermediate), discusses re-usable services and sub processes. It also covers how the processes can get back to the customer, asking for more information related to regulatory requirements, which then gets verified before the process moves to the next level in the approval chain.

Integrating with business partners (Advanced), following on from the concepts covered in the previous recipe, in this recipe we will be taking a closer look at Oracle Service Bus integration with BPM and access partner services.

Collaborating with customers and end users (Simple), shows how customers and process participants collaborate in a portal environment on web and mobile devices. It covers the bigger picture of enterprise, which comprises not only of business process but also various decision-making reports and context-based documents related to the business.

What you need for this book

- ► Oracle Database, Oracle Sun JDK, Oracle JDeveloper IDE, and SQL Developer
- ► Oracle RCU (Repository creation utility), Oracle Weblogic Server
- ► Oracle SOA Suite (includes BPM)
- ► Oracle Webcenter Spaces (optional), Webcenter Content (optional)
- ► SOA BPM Extension for JDeveloper
- ► Oracle Service Bus

Who this book is for

The book is for Java/SOA/BPM Developers and Architects, and is also for people working in financial services in various roles such as Process Administrator/Developer/Business Process Owner or Process Participant. This book helps readers in understanding how BPM can help with financial services scenario at various business roles. The book is not a BPM Developer's Guide, and will not be going deep down into the development methodology. However sufficient information related to how-to activities are provided so that the reader can try these recipes hands on. The book assumes that the reader has a basic knowledge of SOA/BPM/Software Development.

Conventions

In this book, you will find a number of styles of text that distinguish between different kinds of information. Here are some examples of these styles, and an explanation of their meaning.

Code words in text are shown as follows: "Right-click on the `Loan Application` initiator task and add a counter mark".

New terms and **important words** are shown in bold. Words that you see on the screen, in menus or dialog boxes for example, appear in the text like this: "We can click on the **Properties** tab to enable formatting of text on the x and y axis. We can also select themes or create calculated fields depending on the nature of the report requirements."

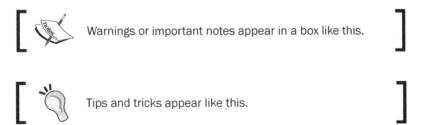

Warnings or important notes appear in a box like this.

Tips and tricks appear like this.

Reader feedback

Feedback from our readers is always welcome. Let us know what you think about this book—what you liked or may have disliked. Reader feedback is important for us to develop titles that you really get the most out of.

To send us general feedback, simply send an e-mail to feedback@packtpub.com, and mention the book title via the subject of your message.

If there is a book that you need and would like to see us publish, please send us a note in the **SUGGEST A TITLE** form on www.packtpub.com or e-mail suggest@packtpub.com.

If there is a topic that you have expertise in and you are interested in either writing or contributing to a book, see our author guide on www.packtpub.com/authors.

Customer support

Now that you are the proud owner of a Packt book, we have a number of things to help you to get the most from your purchase.

Errata

Although we have taken every care to ensure the accuracy of our content, mistakes do happen. If you find a mistake in one of our books—maybe a mistake in the text or the code—we would be grateful if you would report this to us. By doing so, you can save other readers from frustration and help us improve subsequent versions of this book. If you find any errata, please report them by visiting http://www.packtpub.com/support, selecting your book, clicking on the **errata submission form** link, and entering the details of your errata. Once your errata are verified, your submission will be accepted and the errata will be uploaded on our website, or added to any list of existing errata, under the Errata section of that title. Any existing errata can be viewed by selecting your title from http://www.packtpub.com/support.

Piracy

Piracy of copyright material on the Internet is an ongoing problem across all media. At Packt, we take the protection of our copyright and licenses very seriously. If you come across any illegal copies of our works, in any form, on the Internet, please provide us with the location address or website name immediately so that we can pursue a remedy.

Please contact us at copyright@packtpub.com with a link to the suspected pirated material.

We appreciate your help in protecting our authors, and our ability to bring you valuable content.

Questions

You can contact us at questions@packtpub.com if you are having a problem with any aspect of the book, and we will do our best to address it.

Instant Oracle BPM for Financial Services How-to

Welcome to *Instant Oracle BPM for Financial Services How-to*. **Oracle BPM** is a key product of Oracle Fusion Middleware. It helps in automating the enterprise business process. A business process can be modeled by a process analyst. Some of the complex integration and processing logic can be implemented by the IT department. BPM helps the business and IT teams to work together in collaboration with each other towards organization's business goals. BPM also helps the business process owners or the people who have funded and invested in the organization to take key business decisions based on various reports and analysis.

Financial services are becoming highly competitive, and *customer satisfaction* is a critical factor for its survival and growth. In this book, we take a closer look at financial services from an industry point of view, and discuss how BPM can help people at various roles to overcome the challenges faced by them.

Setting up the development environment (Simple)

Financial services are organizations or business houses that are associated with money management, such as investment banks or commercial banks, insurance companies, mortgaging and stock brokerage firms. Some of the major concerns and challenges that these financial services face revolve around security, customer satisfaction, process management, business process administration, partner and customer relationship management, and so on. We will look at some of these challenges from a business point of view.

- ▶ **Security**: Security is a major challenge in financial services that involves keeping customers' money safe and secured. It is necessary to ensure transactional security while customers use their credit cards, debit cards, or do online banking over the Web or through wireless mobile devices.

- ▶ **Customer satisfaction**: Customer satisfaction is also a key factor for financial services. Most banks provide services such as personal loans, home loans, commercial loans, gold loans, mortgage loans, and wealth management consultation. The turnaround period from applying for a loan to getting cash in hand has to be kept as short as possible, to ensure maximum customer satisfaction.

- ▶ **Profit margins**: Profit margins are very thin, but are a major requirement for the survival and growth of these organizations. Most often, they operate with their own funds. Sometimes they might even borrow money from other lenders or banks at a lower rate of interest and give the same money to their customers at a higher rate of interest.

- ▶ **Payment processing**: Payments can happen over the Web, through mobile devices, using credit/debit cards, and so on. They also need to ensure that transactions are authentic and non-fraudulent by sending notifications on debiting/crediting or duplicate billing in an account, and by escalating and blocking an account when illegal access attempts are made.

- ▶ **Follow regulatory and compliance requirements**: Every country has its own local and international trade laws that financial services need to follow. They also need to preserve documents and records for a certain period of time.

Getting ready

Before proceeding further, we need to set up our development environment. For that, we need to have a desktop machine or a laptop with the Windows or Linux operating system installed. It is preferable to have a 64-bit operating system with more than 4-GB RAM. Alternatively, if you have access, you can use an Oracle SOA BPM WebCenter pre-installed virtual machine, or you can configure one yourself.

The full list of software packages required is as follows:

▸ Oracle Database, Oracle JDK, Oracle JDeveloper IDE, and Oracle SQL Developer

▸ Oracle Repository Creation Utility (RCU) and Oracle WebLogic Server

▸ Oracle SOA Suite (includes BPM)

▸ Oracle WebCenter Spaces (optional) and Oracle WebCenter Content (optional)

▸ SOA and BPM extensions for JDeveloper

> The demos and examples used in this book are developed on the Fedora 17 Linux operating system (64-bit) having 12-GB RAM and 6-core processor with Oracle Database 11g Release 1 installed on it, and running the following software packages:
>
> ▸ Oracle JDK (1.6.0_30)
>
> ▸ Oracle RCU (11.1.1.6.0)
>
> ▸ Oracle WebLogic Server 11g Release 1 (10.3.6)
>
> ▸ Oracle SOA Suite 11g Release 1 PS5 (11.1.1.6.0) that includes BPM as well
>
> ▸ Oracle WebCenter Spaces 11g Release 1 (11.1.1.6.0) configured with BPM Process Spaces
>
> ▸ Oracle WebCenter Content 11g Release 1 (11.1.1.6.0)
>
> ▸ Oracle Service Bus PS5 (11.1.1.6.0)

How to do it...

In this recipe, we will configure a WebLogic domain to include Oracle WebCenter Portal with BPM Process Spaces, so that we can use WebCenter Portal to access BPM process-related process tasks and monitor the process. The commands that we run in this recipe use a system name of james on a Linux-based operating system.

1. Launch the terminal and run the following command:

```
cd /home/james/Oracle/Middleware/Oracle_SOA1/common/bin
[james@james bin]$ ./config.sh
```

This will launch the domain configuration wizard. Select the option to create a new Domain.

2. Select **Oracle WebCenter Spaces**, **Oracle BPM Suite for developers**, **Oracle SOA Suite for developers**, **Oracle Universal Content Management**, **Oracle BAM**, and **Oracle Enterprise Manager**. Once you have done that, click on **Next**.

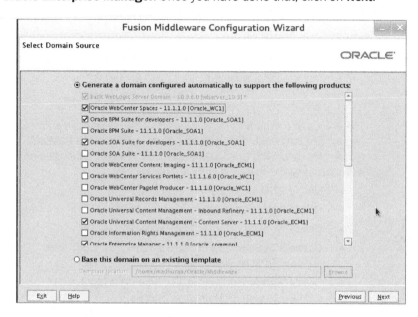

3. Select all the component schemas and give the corresponding DBMS/ service names, database port numbers, and schema passwords. Once you have done that, click on **Next**.

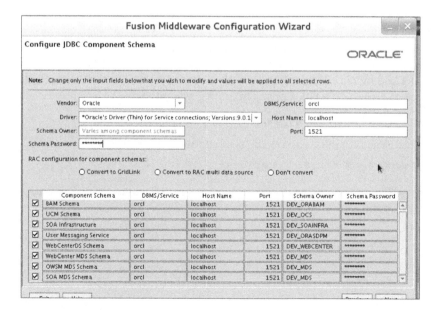

4. Create a domain with the name `fmw_domain`, and then click on **Finish**.

5. Once again launch the domain creation wizard, and this time extend `fmw_domain` and patch it up with the `oracle.bpm.spaces_template_11.1.1.jar` template to enable BPM Process Spaces within WebCenter.

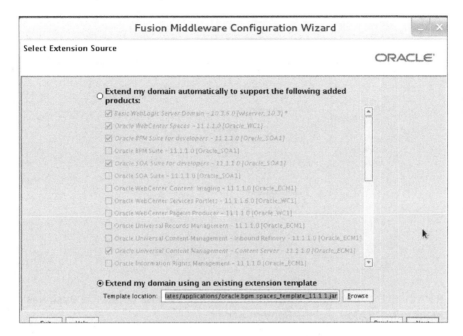

6. Edit `process-portal-install.properties` in the `/home/james/Oracle/Middleware/Oracle_SOA1/bpm/process_spaces` folder, and run the Ant script as shown in following command:

```
/home/james/Oracle/Middleware/modules/org.apache.ant_1.7.1/bin/ant
-f install.xml
```

7. Log in to Enterprise Manager (`http://localhost:7001/em`) and configure Content Server with its default intradoc server port, **4444**, and a UCM connection in WebCenter.

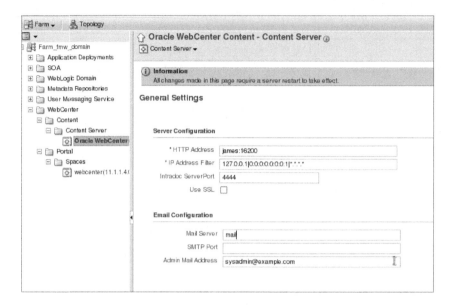

8. Restart all the Managed Servers, Admin Server, WebCenter, Oracle **Business Activity Monitoring** (**BAM**), and the Content Server.

 Please change the commands used in this recipe according to your system name and installation folders.

How it works...

Log in to WebCenter Portal at `http://localhost:8888/webcenter` and ensure that the BPM Process Spaces group space is working, and that we are able to access documents in the content repository. Also, this can be a good time to start working on creating a WebCenter Portal template and WebCenter Portal navigation.

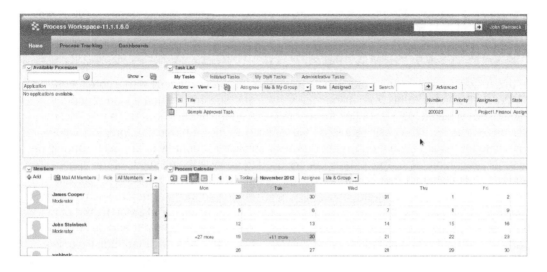

There's more...

This book showcases a home loan use case from build to deployment and from run to manage. It would also be interesting to know that Oracle has **process accelerators**—a prebuilt, "ready to deploy" BPM process that meets industry standards. These process accelerators not only use Oracle BPM, but other Oracle products as well, depending on the business requirements. There are two types of process accelerators:

- **Horizontal process accelerators**: These are process accelerators that can be re-used across any industry where they help streamline business processes. Some examples include travel request management, document routing and approval, internal service requests, and so on.

- **Industry process accelerators**: These are specifically designed for a particular industry. Examples include Public Sector Incident Reporting, Financial Services Loan Origination Process, and so on. Some of these accelerators are purely BPM based, and some integrate with other Oracle applications as well, depending on the business requirements.

Modeling a home loan business process (Intermediate)

In this recipe, we will partially model and simulate a business process with a core focus on **Oracle Business Rules** from a financial services perspective. In home loan scenarios, a customer is asked to fill an online form or talk to a financial advisor at the bank. These discussions capture the basic required dataset such as the loan purpose, property value, loan amount required, loan repayment duration, applicant's monthly or annual income, type of employment, and age. These datasets are used to analyze the eligibility of the applicant, and to find out whether they qualify for the requested loan amount. Banks often classify their customers into Gold/Platinum customers based on various parameters such as annual income, loyalty with the bank for existing customers, and transactional amount. The primary focus in this recipe is to check if the person is within the eligible age limit and belongs to a particular income group based on which customers are classified into Platinum, Gold, Silver, and Bronze customers. The people who do not meet the required age group or income group are considered as not eligible.

 Many screen captures, deployment- and configuration-related steps are not shown in detail in this book. However, these are made available in the ready-to-use source code and on my blog (jamessmith73.wordpress. com) under the *BPM for Financial Services* section.

Getting ready

We will start with a ready-made schema, available in the source code that is used to check the eligibility of an applicant. This recipe need JDeveloper and a running SOA Suite instance. Download the recipe's source code and take a look at the jamesbank.xsd schema file from the source code folder for request and response elements.

How to do it...

Let's perform the following steps:

1. Launch JDeveloper and create a new BPM application.
2. Name the application as JamesBank and then click on **Next**.
3. Name the project as LoanEligibilityProj and then click on **Next**.

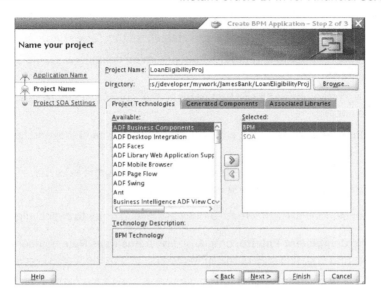

4. In **Project SOA Settings**, select **Composite with BPMN Process**.

5. Select **Synchronous Service** and name it as `LoanEligibilityProcess`.

6. Change to the BPM Project Navigation view and select `LoanEligibilityProcess`.

7. Create a business object and name it as `EligibilityBO`. Create a new destination module and name it as `Module`. Select **Based on External Schema**; this schema then needs to be picked from the schema browser. This is where we need to pick up `eligibilityRequest` from the `jamesbank.xsd` schema file.

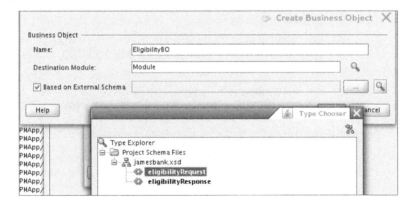

 Ensure that the XSD file is copied into the project from the external directory.

8. Similarly, create another business object and name it as `EligibilityRespBO`. This maps to the `eligibilityResponse` element of the `jamesbank.xsd` schema.

9. Now we need to create input and output argument definitions. Name the input arguments as `inputArgs`.

10. Similarly, create `outputArgs` that maps to the `EligibilityRespBO` business object.

11. Under **Process Data Objects**, create a new process data object and name it as `EligibilityPDO`.

12. Similarly, create `EligibilityRespPDO` that maps to the `Module.EligibilityRespBO` component.

Now perform the following steps to create a business rule in order to check eligibility:

1. From the **Component Palette**, drag-and-drop a **Business Rule** component between the start and end activities of the BPM process and name it as `EligibilityRule`.

2. Create a new business rule by clicking on the **+** icon to the right of the **Business Rule** field and name it as `EligibilityBR`.

3. Pass input and output parameters from the process data objects.

4. Edit the business rule in the Rules Editor:

    1. Create a decision table, name it as `EligibilityDecisionTable`, and then click on **Bucketsets** from the left tab.

    2. Enter the age range, monthly income range, and loan range discussed as follows:
        - The age ranges will be less than 18, 18 to 50, and greater than 50 years
        - The monthly income ranges will be less than 30,000, between 30,000 to 60,000, between 60,000 to 100,000, and greater than 100,000 INR
        - The loans range will be less than 1,000,000, between 1,000,000 to 5,000,000, and greater than 5,000,000 INR

    3. Select global variables by clicking on **Globals** from the left tab in the Rules Editor.

    4. Select `EligibilityRule`, set the rule conditions, and then assign values based on it.

We will now understand the rule modeling in the decision table.

▶ The next screenshot shows `EligibilityDecisionTable` where applicants with age group less than 18 and greater than 50 years are marked as **"NE"** (not eligible). Applicants who are in the eligible age group are classified into various categories based on the monthly income and the loan amount requested.

- In the decision table, we will ignore people with age range less than 18 and greater than 50 years and mark them as **"NE"** in the response status.

- The people with monthly income less than 30,000 INR are also marked as **"NE"**.

- This leaves us with the people between the age group 18 and 50 years and loan applicants with monthly income greater than 30,000 INR who are marked as eligible.

- The applicants with a monthly income greater than 100,000 INR and a loan request greater than 5,000,000 INR are the people who are core customers for the success of, let's say, **"James Bank"**. So we set them as **"Platinum"** customers in `EligibilityRespPDO`.

- The rest of the eligible customers (applicants) fall under the **"Gold"**, **"Silver"**, and **"Bronze"** categories.

- We can then calculate fixed and variable EMI amounts based on the EMI calculation formulas.

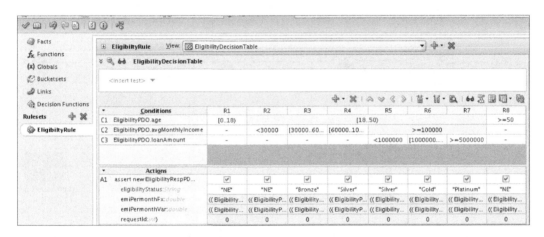

Now that our business rules are ready, we will add them into the process in order to check applicant's eligibility.

How it works...

Bucketsets allow us to define a range of values to be used in the business rules. In the bucketset, we created the ranges for age, monthly income, and the requested loan ranges.

Global variables are the variables that are available within the business rule, which can be even changed during runtime by the process analyst in the business process. We will now create two global variables—one for fixed rate of interest EMIs and another for variable rate of interest EMIs. Fixed interest rate and variable interest rate are the variables that will hold these interest rates as their values.

The process flow and the model (shown in the next screenshot) for the `LoanEligibility` business process modeling is summarized as follows:

1. The user submits a loan request at the **Start** event.

2. `EligibilityRule` gets fired. This determines various rule parameters based on the business rule defined in the previous section.

3. A decision is made as to whether the applicant is eligible or not. If the applicant is not eligible, the process ends.

4. If the applicant is a Platinum customer, a special discount is offered and a notification is sent to the loan officer as a heads up.

5. If the customer is from the Platinum, Gold, Silver, or Bronze category, then the process moves ahead for further modeling, which will be discussed in next recipe. At this stage, we can leave that as a "not implemented" activity or mark it as **Is Draft**.

6. Deploy the business process to SOA Administration Server.

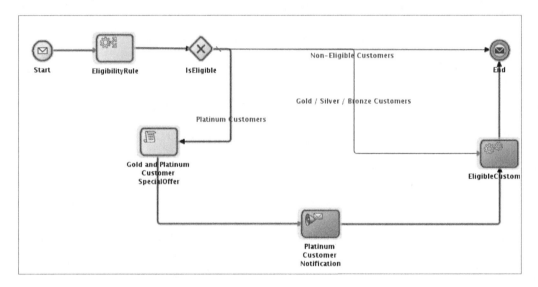

We will now simulate our home loan business process to check how it works so far:

1. Let us log in to Enterprise Manager (`http://localhost:7001/em`) as `weblogic`, and run the process by selecting `LoanEligibilityProj`.

 Replace the URL with your hostname or IP address if it is not `localhost` or using any other port.

2. Provide the following test inputs:

   - ❑ **Property City**: Bangalore
   - ❑ **Loan Request Amount**: 7500000
   - ❑ **Loan Purpose**: Home Loan
   - ❑ **Market Value of Property**: 9500000
   - ❑ **Repayment Duration in months**: 60
   - ❑ **Applicant Age**: 30
   - ❑ **Employment Type**: Salaried
   - ❑ **Company Name**: JS Bank
   - ❑ **Average Monthly Income**: 150000

The output of this process will be a Platinum customer, which can be viewed from the **Audit Trail** and **Flow** tabs. The green line in the flow denotes a *happy path* or the path taken by the process for the given input data.

There's more...

Business rules not only support decision tables, but also **if-then conditions**. The same rule can be modeled as: *if* the customer age is less than 18, *then* assign the eligibility status as not eligible. It's a matter of choice whether you use decision tables or if-then conditions. Decision tables support complex business logic within business rules when compared to if-then conditions.

Implementing a home loan business process (Advanced)

A **process analyst** needs to have expertise on BPMN 2.0 models. They should also be able to understand the business process and business rules, collaborate with other business users, and simulate and document the process. It is also expected that a process analyst can model and edit the process on runtime using BPM Composer if there are changes in the business requirements. Oracle BPM allows process analysts to monitor the process, or even assign a given task to any user in the workflow system. BPM's out of the box integration capabilities allows analysts to view or check-in documents from or into the content repository related to his process.

A **process developer** needs to have expertise on BPMN 2.0 models from a technical point of view and the ability to write complex business logic in Java or PL/SQL. If required, he needs to have expertise in implementing the process model itself, by integrating with the necessary applicants or legacy systems by using BPM or SOA.

This recipe continues from the previous process model and implements the eligible customers business logic.

Getting ready

Before we begin, the following requirement needs to be fulfilled:

- ▸ Download the source code from the previous recipe.
- ▸ Use Oracle SQL Developer to develop and test a stored procedure to compute the EMI amount. We can use the SQL scripts provided in the code files of this recipe to create the database user and execute the procedure.
- ▸ Ensure that SOA Suite is running.

Let us understand how a home loan EMI is calculated. Home loan EMI's are calculated based on the following formula:

EMI = (L*I)* {(1+I)^N / [(1+I)^N]-1}

Where:

L = Requested loan amount

I = Interest rate (rate per annum divided by 12)

^ = To the power of

N = Repayment duration in months

So, assuming a loan of 100,000 INR at 11 percent per annum that is repayable in 15 years, which is 180 months, the EMI using the formula will be:

EMI = (100000*0.00916)* {(1+0.00916)^180 / [(1+0.00916)^180]-1}

EMI ~ 916 * (5.161846 / 4.161846)

EMI ~ 1,136 INR

How to do it...

We need to create a PL/SQL procedure that can calculate fixed and variable EMIs, and also generate a unique request ID for every eligibility request. We will be passing the interest rate (*I*) to the PL/SQL procedure from the BPM business rules.

Writing a business logic in PL/SQL and integrating it with the process is done as follows:

1. Log in to Oracle Database as the SYS user.
2. Create the JAMESBANKDB user and grant all the required create table, create trigger, and create sequence privileges to this user.
3. Log in as JAMESBANKDB.

4. Create the procedure to calculate EMIs and write the data in the database table.

> The SQL scripts are available in the code files for this recipe.

5. **Compile** and **Run** the `Insert Eligibility` procedure. This procedure will insert the eligibility data into a table, calculate the EMI amount for fixed and variable rate of interest, and also return a unique ID for the eligibility request.

6. Launch JDeveloper and open the James Bank application developed in the previous recipe.

7. Open `composite.xml` in the **Design** view.

8. In the **External References** area on right side in the **Design** view, insert a **Database Adapter** service.

9. Set up the necessary database connection parameters:

    ❑   **Connection Name**: `jamesbankdb`

    ❑   **Username**: `jamesbankdb`

    ❑   **Password**: `welcome1`

    ❑   **JDBC Port**: `1521`

    ❑   **Service Name**: `orcl`

10. Test the connection and proceed if it is successful.

11. In the Adapter Configuration Wizard, select the **Call a Stored Procedure or Function** operation type.

12. From the configuration wizard, select the `EMI Calculator` stored procedure.

13. Open the `LoanEligibility` process in the **Design** view, and change the `EligibleCustomers` activity into a service task, and make it *active* (earlier it was marked as draft).

14. Select the **Database Adapter** service that we have created in the service list.

15. Now click on **Data Associations** and ensure that the necessary input and output parameters are passed.

16. Save the process and deploy on SOA Suite.

17. Generate a web service-based **Application Development Framework** (**ADF**) data control by using the deployed WSDL URL, and drag-and-drop it on the JSPX page.

18. Right-click and **Run** the JSPX page to test the web service from the browser by giving necessary input parameters, and then clicking on the **Check Eligibility** button, as shown in the next screenshot.

How it works...

We have build a PL/SQL procedure to calculate EMIs, store the necessary input data into the database table, and generate a request ID for every eligible application request. In the James Bank's loan application business rules, we are dynamically passing the fixed and variable interest rate (*I*). We have also built a business logic that defines Platinum, Gold, Silver, Bronze, and NE customers. We then deployed our BPM process. The process can be tested from Enterprise Manager or a simple ADF web service-based data control.

The role clarification process analyst was responsible for creating the dynamic business logic in the BPM process, including business rules, whereas the process developer was responsible for creating the PL/SQL stored procedure for the static business logic. The process developer was also responsible for creating and deploying the ADF application, and implementing some of the process logic as planned by the process analyst.

The output of this recipe is ready to run the home loan EMI calculator application that works on a particular business logic. We also learnt how the business logic in the BPM rules engine communicates through a service invocation with the business logic stored in stored procedures or any other legacy systems.

In the browser UI, enter input values and check for the web service return values, as shown in the following screenshot:

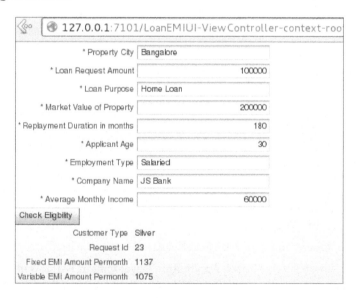

Log in to Enterprise Manager and view the process flow. The major change that we see in the process flow is the business service invocation at the PL/SQL database layer by the BPM process.

Our business logic is now ready to be used in the main Home Loan Process.

There's more...

It would also be interesting to know that BPM supports integration with EJB-written business logic. So if we are not planning to implement PL/SQL-based business logic, we can write the same logic by using EJBs, and invoke it as a BPM service activity. Alternatively, we can also use a combination of BPMN expression language to compute the EMI, and use a simple Database Adapter to write the data into a database table and generate the request ID.

Deploying and testing a process workflow (Advanced)

A **process administrator's** role involves governing, configuring, and maintaining BPM processes and business rules. They are in charge of BPM Server administration, policy management, providing grant access to various users based on their role in the process, and deploying/undeploying the process as and when required by the IT organization, who are directly linked to the business organization unit of James Bank.

Process participants are people who are part of the process and interact with other process participants or customers. They are directly or indirectly involved in moving the process ahead. In James Bank's scenario, Conan Doyle, Jack London, and John Steinbeck are involved in preliminary and secondary loan applicants' credential checks. Some of their work is manual, some automated; but they keep the ball rolling ahead. William Faulkner, who heads the finance organization, is also involved in the final checks and finance approval of the process.

Getting ready

Before we begin, the following requirement needs to be fulfilled:

- ▶ Download the source code from the previous recipe
- ▶ Ensure that the `LoanEligibility` process is deployed and working as expected

Let's use the James Bank's loan schema, `application.xsd`, to create a new BPM project for the loan application. The request and response elements can be seen in application.xsd file provided with the source code of this chapter.

This recipe demonstrates WebCenter Process Spaces. If you already have WebCenter installed with BPM Process Spaces, then we can use WebCenter Portal. If you do not have WebCenter Portal, then we can test the same process in BPM Workspace application as well.

How to do it...

Let us extend the home loan use case based on the following points:

▶ **James Cooper** is the loan applicant who has applied for a home loan. He now knows that he is eligible for loan and has an option of choosing a fixed or variable EMI. He also has a unique loan request ID that will be used throughout his home loan processing. He submits the required document proofs such as property address, government approval of the property, proof of address, salary slips, and his income tax return statements, as required by James' Bank in order to process his loan application.

 Refer to the previous recipe for details about loan eligibility.

▶ The process continues in a parallel mode where application document verification and physical address and employment proofs are checked by field officers.

▶ **Conan Doyle** and **Jack London**—who are in the role of Application Verification Officers—validate the documents such as address proof and salary slips sent by James Cooper. If they are satisfied with the validity of the documents, either one of them approves them. This task is named as **Application Verification Officer**.

▶ **John Steinbeck**—who is in the role of Field Officer—physically visits James Cooper's home and office, and checks his residential address and employment status. When both the Application Verification Officer and the Field Officer—provide their approval, the process moves to the next level. This task is named as **Agency Verification**.

 Sometimes, banks can hire an external agency to verify address, property documents, employment status, and criminal records.

▶ **William Faulkner** is the Finance Officer at James Bank. He would be the final approver in the business process.

▶ Based on the customer's monthly income and the requested loan amount, the loan applicants are classified as Platinum, Gold, Silver, and Bronze customers.

▶ Platinum customers are the ones who have requested a substantial loan amount, and sometimes it makes sense for James Bank to borrow the loan from other partner banks or financial institutions at a lower rate of interest, and give the same loan to their customers at a higher rate of interest. So there is a subprocess that takes care of communicating with partner networks based on certain service-level agreements. This task is named as **Partner Loan Request Process**.

All the users—*James Cooper, Jack London, Conan Doyle*, and *John Steinbeck*—need to be created in UCM as well. WebCenter Content can be accessed at `http://localhost:16200/cs`. If not created, these users would not be able to check documents in to the content repository.

Let us now model this process in JDeveloper by performing the following steps:

1. Launch JDeveloper and create a new project under the James Bank application. Name this project as `LoanApplicationProj`.

2. Create input arguments, output arguments, business objects, and business process data objects.

3. Map all the request objects to the `loanRequest` element of the schema, and map all the response elements to the `loanResponse` element of the schema.

4. Create `LoanApplicant`, `VerificationOfficer`, `FieldOfficer`, and `FinanceOfficer` swimlanes on the process canvas, which can be seen in the extreme left vertical lane in the **Flow** tab. Each of these represents a participant role.

5. Switch to the **BPM Project Navigator** view and open the **Organizational Chart** roles. Add the required actors as discussed in the preceding use case for each of the swimlane roles.

6. Drag-and-drop a task initiator from the **Component Palette** on the `LoanApplicant` BPM process swimlane.

7. Create the `Loan Application` human task and associate it with the `loanRequest` process data object as an input parameter.

8. Select `Loan Application Task` and click on **Auto-Generate Task Form...**.

9. Add a parallel task and link up `AgencyVerification` and `Application Verification Officer`, so that they merge again at the `ParallelGateway` endpoint.

10. Add an exclusive gateway to check if the customer is a Platinum customer. If *yes*, take the customer to a subprocess (Partner Loan Request Process) which is marked as **Is Draft**, for later implementation.

11. If the customer is *not* a Platinum customer, then the process moves to the next human task—`Finance Approval`.

12. Save the loan application data in the required database table by using a Database Adapter at the `Save Loan Application` service invocation.

We can implement this logic later, so we will mark it as **Is Draft** (shown in gray color).

13. Finally, send an e-mail notification to the customer by dragging and dropping the **Email** notification activity.

14. Deploy the application to WebLogic Server from JDeveloper.

How it works...

The output of this recipe will run `LoanApplicationProcess`, which goes through a series of checks and approvals before the applicant is notified of his loan status.

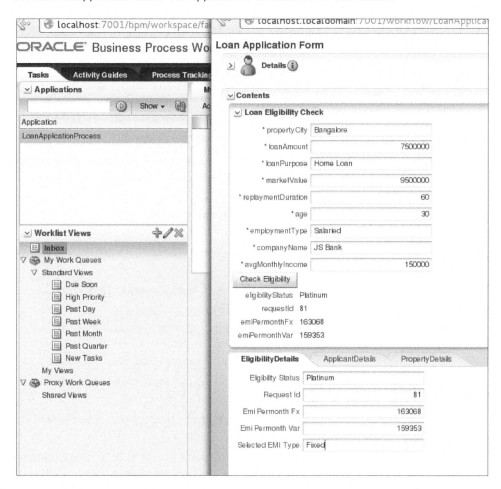

Let's understand how each role in our use case plays its part, by performing the following steps:

1. Log in to BPM Workspace (`http://localhost:7001/bpm/workspace`) as James Cooper (loan applicant).

2. He checks for loan eligibility, fills in the required data, and submits the form.

3. He also attaches required documents such as proof of age, proof of address and salary slips that get checked into the UCM content repository.

4. John Steinbeck—who is the Field Officer—visits James Cooper's home and office, and approves the `Loan Application Task` in the BPM Workspace application.

5. Jack London—who is the Application Verification Officer—has access to the corporate intranet WebCenter Portal. He logs in and verifies all the related documents such as Income Tax **Permanent Account Number** (**PAN**), address proof, and employment certificate and provides his approval on them.

6. After login, he selects his group space related to home loans and views the task assigned to him in the process workflow:

7. He then selects `Application Verification Task` assigned to him and verifies the documents. Once done, he clicks on the **Approve** or **Reject** button to approve or reject the application based on his verification of the documents.

8. William Faulkner—who is the Finance Officer at James Bank—gives the final approval, and the loan is sanctioned to James Cooper.

The following screenshot shows how the end-to-end process flow looks in the Enterprise Manager. The green line shows the *happy path*.

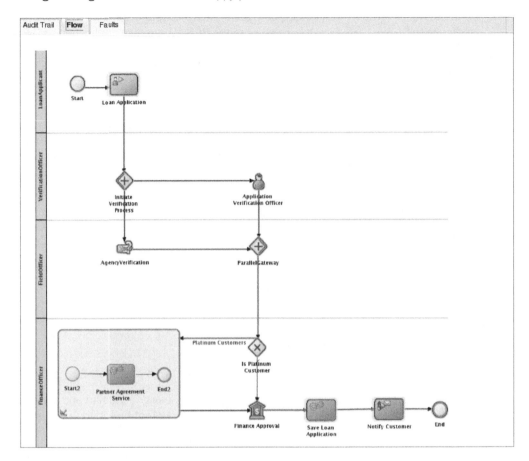

There's more...

Deployments can be done directly from JDeveloper by creating a WebLogic Application Server connection. After deployment, it is necessary to create a data source and a connection pool in the WebLogic Server console. The deployed SOA application can be tested in multiple ways; the most common being to log in to Enterprise Manager and test the process from there. Another approach is to use the web service WSDL URL to create an ADF-based data control. Once created, drag-and-drop this control onto an ADF JSPX page and test it by running the JSPX page. Enterprise Manager-based testing will always be a quicker approach during development stages.

Administering processes (Advanced)

Process escalation is one of the core features of BPM. Suppose if Conan Doyle is on leave or has not approved a task in a given time. The process automatically escalates the task to his manager or some other user in the business process, so that the task continues on time, according to their service-level agreements.

The following are some of the other important features of BPM:

- ▶ **Document management capabilities**: BPM's out of the box integration capabilities allow process documents to be checked-in directly to the content repository (UCM). These documents are carried across the process workflow and are visible to all the process participants.

- ▶ **Setting deadlines**: BPM allows task expiry based on a certain time interval. By default, tasks never expire. Sometimes, there can be a business case where James Bank offers festival discounts to its customers , and these can expire and become inactive after a certain time interval.

- ▶ **Process simulation**: This is another key area that allows the business analyst to make some important decisions based on time, effort, and cost analysis. Process simulation can help in calculating return on investment benefits.

Getting ready

Before we begin, the following requirement needs to be fulfilled:

- ▶ Download the source code from the previous recipe.
- ▶ Ensure that WebCenter Content, WebCenter Portal, and SOA Suite are running. Also ensure that the process is running as expected, end to end.

How to do it...

Without any more delay, let's perform the following steps:

1. Launch JDeveloper and open the `Application Verification Task` human task.
2. Click on the **Deadlines** tab, and in the **Task Duration Settings** field, change the value of the **Escalate after** drop-down list to 7 days.
3. To set up an escalation rule, from the **Task Duration Settings** field, select the **Expires after** drop-down list and then in the **Fixed Duration** drop-down list, set the value to 5 working days. One can also set the escalation process to notify the manager if no action is taken within a specified time.

4. We can also set up document management capabilities for the document that has been checked in. To do this, enable the document package under the documents tab.

5. In this process, we will set `AgencyVerification` to have a fixed cost of $100. Similarly, we can set up a number of process instances to be simulated based on time and cost on a given task.

To create a simulation model, let's perform the following steps:

1. In JDeveloper, click on the **BPM Project Navigator** tab.

2. Then under **Simulations**, create a new simulation model named `LoanSimulationModel`.

3. Save the simulation model.

4. Create a new simulation definition named `LoanSimulationDefinition` based on the current simulation model. We can also specify start and end times, and there can also be multiple processes simulated in one simulation definition.

 In a real business scenario, we need to make some assumptions related to the time taken by each role and the corresponding cost involved in each stage of the process. We can also configure whether the cost is on a per-hour basis or is fixed for a given task or activity for a certain role.

5. Run the simulation model by clicking on the *green run button* located in the process simulation taskbar below the process canvas.

How it works...

We can view the process flow under the Simulation mode. We can also change to a 3-dimensional display of the simulated process. The display shows current instances, and instances in the queue waiting at various stages for verification or approvals.

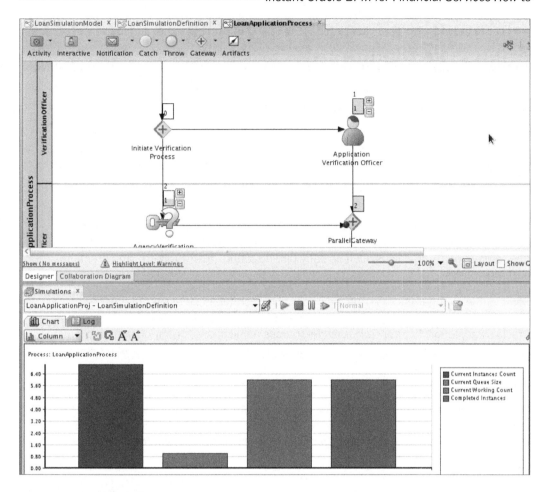

There's more...

It is also possible to include multiple business processes under one simulation definition, and estimate the total cost and the time factor. We can also add the Partner Quote Business Process, discussed later in the *Integrating with business partners* recipe, to the current simulation, and estimate the total cost and time to complete a loan approval. These simulation models help process owners to identify process bottlenecks and estimations, in order to set up service-level agreements with their customers.

Changing a business process by the process analyst (Advanced)

Another important feature of BPM is **change management**. The business often changes, and most of these changes are done by the process analyst in line with their current business requirements.

If we look at our home loan use case, the changes that happen almost on a regular basis are changes in the rate of interest. Other changes could be changes in the business flow itself. For example, loans higher than a certain amount may need the Reserve or Federal Bank authority's approval.

There might also be a new compliance requirement where an external auditor would need to be informed before loans are disbursed to loan applicants. Banks can also offer promotional campaigns such as early bird discounts, festival offers, and premium customer offers.

Some of the changes can be IT based or depend upon the business requirements. IT-based changes can be an integration with a new leave application or CRM application, Oracle's PeopleSoft Enterprise Human Resources applications, or any custom applications. The challenge in both the cases would be to ensure business continuity with minimum or no downtime.

In a complex business process, it becomes important to monitor the progress of the process at any given instant in time. This is very important from the point of view of a process owner, process participant, and process initiator (loan applicant in our use case). BPM comes up with a graphical view of **audit trail** capabilities and **standard dashboards** that help in process monitoring and analysis.

Getting ready

Before we begin, the following requirement needs to be fulfilled:

*   Download the source code from the previous recipe and deploy it on the Oracle BPM Metadata Services (MDS) repository that stores changes and customizations.
*   Ensure that BPM Suite is running, along with other Managed Servers such as WebCenter Portal and WebCenter Content.

How to do it...

Let's perform the following steps:

1. Launch JDeveloper and open **BPM MDS Navigator** from the **View** menu.
2. Configure a new BPM MDS connection.

3. Create a database connection with username as DEV_MDS and password as welcome1, and test the connection.

4. Similarly, select the application server connection that we created earlier during the process deployment, and set the MDS partition to obpm. Again, test the connection

5. Select the connection for the **SOA MDS** section and test the BPM MDS connection.

6. In the BPM Project Navigator view, right-click on the project and save LoanApplicationProj to BPM MDS.

7. Log in to BPM Composer as the weblogic user and select the LoanEligibilityProj project.

8. Open the EligibilityBR business rule. Here we can update the business rules as required or add new conditions.

9. To change a business rule, select the **Globals** tab where we have defined fixed and variable rate of interests.

10. Now edit the rate of interests. We will change the fixed rate of interest from 12 percent per annum to 14 percent, and change the variable rate of interest from 10 percent per annum to 12 percent:

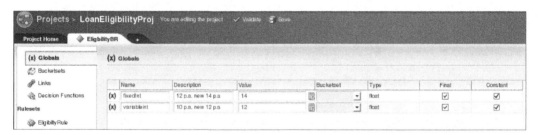

We can also make changes to the business process. Let's say we were previously offering special discounts to our Platinum customers only. Now the business has decided to offer the same discounts to the Gold customers as well.

11. Select the LoanEligibility business process. Then select the condition of Platinum customers and rename this as Gold and Platinum customers.

12. Edit the condition and make changes to it to include Gold customers as well. The condition will be eligibility status == "Platinum" or eligibility status == "Gold". This can be defined by using Expression Builder.

13. Validate the changes and then click on the **Save** button. Now our business changes have been done. The changes need to be deployed from BPM Composer.

Remember to click on **Apply Changes** when done with the changes before saving and deployment.

How it works...

To see the changes, we can input the loan eligibility data from the web user interface or from Enterprise Manager itself. Once the process gets executed, we can view the flow based on the changes that were made. In our case, we have made Gold and Platinum customers both eligible for discount, whereas earlier only Platinum customers were eligible for discount. Also, the rates of interest for both fixed and variable interest rates were increased, impacting the EMI numbers.

The output of this recipe will use the business process that has changes driven by business. We will also look into the audit trail and monitor the process.

Log in to Enterprise Manager as the `weblogic` user. Test the process and view the process flow. It should show the new `LoanEligibility` process deployed and available for our main Home Loan Process.

To view the audit trail of any business process, log in to BPM Workspace as a WebLogic process administrator and click on the **Process Tracking** tab. Select one of the running instances of the process. We will then be able to see how far the process has moved, and whose approval is pending. The lines in green in the following screenshot shows the path completed so far:

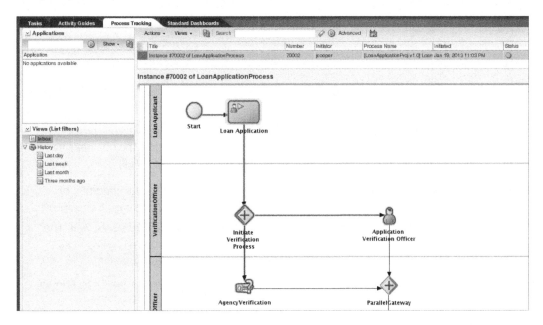

When we first deployed the `LoanEligibility` process from JDeveloper, it was version 1.0. When the same process was saved to BPM MDS, and was edited and redeployed by the process analyst, it became version 1.1. The developer needs to download the latest version by *checking out* from MDS. These processes are editable by only one person at any given point of time.

There's more...

In addition to the standard process flows and audit trails, one can also view standard dashboards. Some of the standard BPM reports are: workload per process, performance per process, and process performance per participant that are out of the box. This will also help the business owner to decide how the resources are getting utilized as well.

Process versioning has an advantage that it is always possible to roll back to a previous version. It is a good practice to not overwrite a stable business process, but instead to create a new version of the same process.

It is also a best practice to have a service layer such as OSB when exposing a process to other services. This avoids external services directly referring to a service that is constantly changing. OSB also provides the capability to add a layer of security and monitoring that would be beneficial when exposing services to the outside world. We will look into OSB in detail later in the *Integrating with business partners* recipe.

Creating business reports for process owners (Intermediate)

Business process owners are C-level and top executives; the people who might have been directly involved in funding or reporting to the board of directors, or the people who are held directly responsible for the overall business performance. They understand, own, and run the business. Their business can be spread into different geographical locations with different lines of business coming under their enterprise. They will be interested in real-time dashboards, business intelligence, and take key decisions based on key performance indicators and other metrics.

BPM has out of the box integration with the BAM application that enables business process participants and process owners to view real-time dashboards. They can also use WebCenter Portal with its out of the box integration capabilities, along with Oracle Business Intelligence Enterprise Edition 11*g* (OBI EE), to view and analyze and take decisions on some of the most complex multidimensional reports.

From a business process, we can capture process-specific data that makes business sense. Some of the terminologies that need to be understood are:

- **Measurements**: Measurements are numerical data. They are basically numbers that make sense in a business process report. For example, a requested loan amount or age group of people can be one of the required measurement fields.
- **Dimensions**: Dimensions are an indication of how the data might be sliced. For example, lower income group, higher income group, middle income group, and so on.
- **Counters**: Counters simply indicate a count in the process. For example, the number of applications in a given month.

Some of the measurements and dimensions that we are going to use are tabulated as follows:

Measurement name	Description
Requested loan amount measurement	This maps to the requested loan amount that was entered by the applicant during the eligibility check
Repayment duration measurement	This maps to the repayment period that was given during the eligibility check
Dimension name	**Description**
Income group dimension	The range is set as follows: ▸ Low-income group from up to 30,000 INR ▸ Average-income group from 30,000 to 60,000 INR ▸ High-income group from 60,000 to 200,000 INR ▸ Very-high income group above 200,000 INR Similarly, we can create a few more dimensions such as customer type dimension and company name dimension, depending on the business requirements.

From a business reporting requirement point of view, some the reports that make sense from a home loan perspective are:

- Number of loan applications in a given period of time
- Number of applications that are at various stages of approval, pending approval, or rejected
- Complete data view of all loan applications
- Income group of loan applicants that can be high-, middle-, and lower-income group
- The loan requested amount for a given period of time
- Changes in fixed and variable rate of interests
- Total amount of loan approved in a given quarter of a month and comparing those with the previous quarter

Getting ready

Before we begin, the following requirements need to be fulfilled:

- Download the source code from the previous recipe.
- Start SOA Suite and the BAM servers. As BAM Web UI is visible on Windows using Internet Explorer, we need a Windows machine with IE7 or 8 installed to view these reports and the BAM application.

 Do check the BAM requirement specifications.

- It is assumed that Database Adapters and BAM Adapters have already been configured in Enterprise Manager.

We will add a simple Database Adapter, `Get Eligibility Details`, that fetches eligibility data based on the request ID of the applicant through an SQL query, as follows:

```
select PROPERTYCITY, LOANAMOUNT, LOANPURPOSE, MARKETVALUE,
REPLAYMENTDURATION, AGE, EMPLOYMENTTYPE, COMPANYNAME,
AVERAGEMONTHLYINCOME, CUSTTYPE, FIXEDEMI, VARIABLEEMI, REQUESTID from
ELIGIBILITYDATA where REQUESTID = ?
```

We will add a service task activity on `LoanApplicationProcess` that invokes the `Get Eligibility Details` Database Adapter. We can name this service activity as `Get Applicants Eligibility Details`.

How to do it...

We will now modify the process to add BAM data object based dimensions and measurements, and also use the BAM application to create a process dashboard.

We will select the home loan business process and add an application counter that counts the number of times the process has been executed. We can put this at the start of the process, or just while the loan application is initiated by James Cooper. To do that, let's perform the following steps:

1. Launch JDeveloper and then right-click on the `Loan Application` initiator task and add a counter mark.
2. Assign it to the application counter.

   We will now create the following dimensions and measurements, as discussed earlier at the start of this recipe:

3. Right-click on `LoanApplicationProj` and select **Project Preferences**. Under **Process Analytics Summary**, ensure that **eis/bam/soap** is selected. Also, the **Enable Cubes** and **Enable BAM** checkboxes are selected. We can select the default folder path or select a new path as required.

4. Log in to BAM as the `weblogic` user at `http://localhost:9001/OracleBAM/`.

5. Click on **Architect**. We can now view data in the BAM data objects that got pushed from BPM. Usually, the data object name will be of the form `BI_ default_<project name>_<process name>`. In our case, it will be `BI_ default_LoanApplicationProj_LoanApplicationProcess`.

6. In BAM Active Studio, create the report by selecting a report type and the data objects that holds our BPM data. The **Data** tab shows all the available columns. We can select the one that is needed to generate our report.

7. We can click on the **Properties** tab to enable formatting of text on the x and y axes. We can also select themes, or create calculated fields, depending on the nature of the report requirements.

8. BAM also is capable of sending BAM alerts and notifications that can be configured. For example, we can set up an alert when a fraud is detected during the document verification stage.

How it works...

The output of this recipe uses the business process that is capable of delivering standard and customized business reports to the business process owners and the business analysts. We have created some standard and customized reports that can be viewed in the BAM dashboard.

From the BAM Active Viewer, we can view the standard and customized reports. Some of the customized reports that we have created for the process owners are shown in the following screenshot:

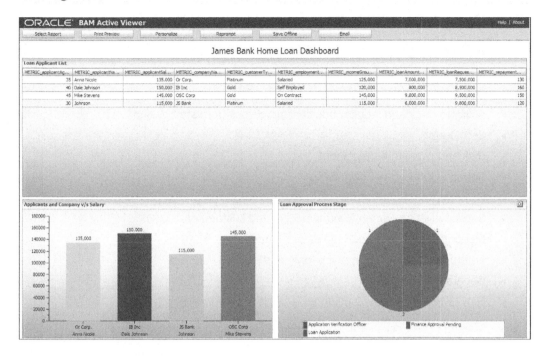

There's more...

It would be interesting to know that BAM presents real-time reports based on data objects that get populated by one or more business processes. On the other hand, BI reports are capable of building reports from multiple data sources such as databases, XML files, Excel files, and historical data. BI reports add a layer of analysis and intelligence on top of an existing dataset. In a real-life financial services scenario, the process owner or the participants can have a combined report view of all BPM standard reports, and BI and BAM reports, on their WebCenter Portal. There can also be user- and context-based reports. Users can also personalize these reports based on their roles.

Participating in a business process (Intermediate)

The key business requirements for financial services from a business point of view are:

- Payment processing
- Transaction management
- Fraud detection
- Ability to track and monitor business processes from start to end
- Escalation
- Risk and change management
- Reduced total cost of ownership
- Higher return on investment
- Service-level agreements with partners and customers
- Meeting compliance and regulatory requirements
- Enterprise growth in terms of people and process volumes
- Geographical expansion
- New diversified businesses under a single enterprise

The hurdles and bottlenecks for financial services from an IT point of view are:

- Silos of data
- Outdated IT system and many applications running on legacy and non-standard based systems
- Business process and reporting systems not in sync with each other
- Lack of real-time data visibility
- Automated decision making
- Ability to change and manage business processes in accordance with changes in business dynamics
- Partner management
- Customer satisfaction

This is where BPM plays a key role in bridging the gap between key business requirements and technology or businesses hurdles.

In a real-life scenario, a typical home loan use case would be tied up with **Know Your Customer** (**KYC**) regulatory requirement. In India for example, the **Reserve Bank of India** (**RBI**) had passed on guidelines that make it mandatory for banks to properly know their customers. RBI mandates that banks collect their customers' proof of identity, recent photographs, and Income Tax PAN. Proof of residence can be a voter card, a driving license, or a passport copy.

Getting ready

We start with the source code from the previous recipe. We will add a re-usable e-mail or SMS notification process. It is always a best practice to add a new process if it is called multiple times in the same process. This can be a subprocess within the main process itself, or it can be a part of the same composite outside the main process. We will add a new regulatory requirement that allows the customer to add KYC requirements such as photo, proof of address, and Income Tax PAN copy as attachments that will be checked into the WebCenter Content repository. These checks become a part of the customer verification stage before finance approval. We will make KYC as a subprocess with a scope of expansion under a different scenario. We will also save the process data into a filesystem or in a JMS messaging queue at the end of the loan process completion. In a banking scenario, it can also be the integration stage for other applications such as a CRM application or any other application.

How to do it...

Let's perform the following steps:

1. Launch JDeveloper and open the `composite.xml` of `LoanApplicationProcess` in the **Design** view.

2. Drag-and-drop a new **BPMN Process** component from the **Component Palette**.

3. Create the `Send Notifications` process next to the existing `LoanApplicationProcess`, and edit the new process.

4. The `Send Notifications` process will take input parameters as To e-mail ID, From e-mail ID, Subject, CC, and send e-mail to the given e-mail ID.

5. Similarly, we will drag-and-drop a **File Adapter** component from the **Component Palette** that saves the customer data into a file. We place this component the end of the `LoanApplication` process, just before the **End** activity.

   We will use this notification service to notify Verification Officers about the arrival of a new eligible application that needs to be verified.

6. In the `Application Verification Officer` stage, we will add a subprocess, `KYC`, that will be assigned to the loan initiator—James Cooper in our case.

7. This will be preceded by sending an e-mail notification to the applicant asking for KYC details such as PAN number, scanned photograph, and voter ID as requested by the Verification Officers.

8. Now, let us implement `Save Loan Application` by invoking the **File Adapter** service. The **Email** notification services are also available out of the box.

How it works...

The outputs of this recipe are re-usable services that can be used across multiple service calls such as notification services. This recipe also demonstrates how to use subprocesses and change the process to meet regulatory requirements.

Let's understand the output by taking our use case scenario:

1. When the process is initiated, the e-mail notification gets triggered at appropriate stages of the process.

2. Conan Doyle and John Steinbeck will get the e-mail, requesting them to process the application, with the required information of the applicant, along with the link to BPM Workspace.

3. The KYC task also sends an e-mail to James Cooper, requesting him for the documents required for the KYC check.

4. James Cooper logs in to the James Bank WebCenter Portal and sees there is a task assigned to him to upload his KYC details.

5. James Cooper clicks on the task link and submits the required soft copy documents, and gets them checked into the content repository once the form is submitted.

The start-to-end process flow now looks as follows:

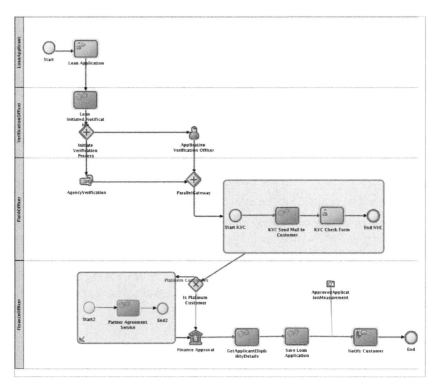

There's more...

BPM Process Spaces, which is an extension template of BPM, allows process and task views to be exposed to WebCenter Portal. The advantage of having Process Spaces made available within the Portal is that the users can collaborate with others using out of the box Portal features such as wikis, discussion forums, blogs, and content management. This improves productivity as the user need not log in to different applications for different purposes, as all the required data and information will be made available within the Portal environment. It is also possible to expose some of the WSRP supported application portlets (for example, HR Portlets from PeopleSoft) into a corporate portal environment. All of this sums up to provide higher visibility of the entire business process, and a nature of working and collaborating together in an enterprise business environment.

Integrating with business partners (Advanced)

Loren Kelleher Bank is a fictitious bank that helps other commercial banks and financial services by providing loans at a lower rate of interest. James Bank has partnered with Loren Kelleher Bank to get loans at a lower rate of interest, and the same funds are disbursed to loan applicants at a higher rate of interest. The difference between the buying rate of interest and the lending rate of interest is what forms a major chunk of James Bank's profit margin. So, it has tied up with many such banks and financial institutions to find out who quotes the lowest rate of interest. Loren Kelleher Bank has a partner service made available on **Oracle Service Bus** (**OSB**) that allows banks such as James Bank and other financial institutions to reach them for a rate of interest quote. It also makes business sense for small- and medium-sized banks such as James Bank to borrow loans at a lower rate of interest, and give the same loan at a higher rate of interest to their customers.

Getting ready

Before we begin, the following requirement needs to be fulfilled:

- ▸ Download the source code from the previous recipe.
- ▸ It's also assumed that OSB is already installed and available. If you do not have OSB available, you can leave this activity as draft.

How to do it...

Let's create an OSB layer service that allows partner banks to send a quote on the rate of interest based on the received loan request.

1. Lets create a simple Partner Business Process, `LorenRateofInterestQuoteProcess`, that accepts loan request input from James Bank's `LoanApplicationProcess` and returns quotes for fixed and variable rates of interest. It also waits for some time before completing the process. This can be considered as a waiting period for the Quote Officer to complete his/her task of sending the quote back.

2. Deploy the process.

3. Log in to Enterprise Manager (`http://localhost:7001/em`) and download the WSDL as `LorenRateofInterestQuoteProcess.service.xml` from the process WSDL URL.

4. To create OSB resources, log in to OSB at `http://localhost:7001/sbconsole`.

5. Create a new project.

6. Under **Change Center** click on the **Create** button.

7. Create a resource of type **WSDL** and upload the `LorenRateofInterestQuoteProcess.service.xml` WSDL file.

8. Similarly, create one more resource of type **XML Schema** and upload the `jamesbankloanapplication.xsd` file.

 The XSD file is available in the source code folder.

9. Create a business service as `PartnerQuoteBusinessService`. This will make an HTTP request to our Partner Business Process that we had deployed. It also makes it easier for the Partner to modify the endpoint URL in case the process gets redeployed into some other machine or into some other WSDL URL.

10. Create a proxy service as `PartnerQuoteProxyService` that maps to `PartnerQuoteBusinessService`. This proxy service uses the **SB** protocol to communicate with a business service.

11. To test the proxy service, click on the **Launch Test Console** icon under the **Actions** column to launch the test console for the proxy service.

12. Provide the required XML input as the request message.

13. Log in to BPM Composer, enter the quote, and we will be able to see the response message in SOAP format.

14. In JDeveloper, open the `composite.xml` file of `LoanApplicationProcess` in the **Design** view.

15. Insert a **Direct Binding** service from the **Component Palette**, as this invokes our OSB layer proxy service.

16. Edit `LoanApplicationProcess` and call the partner service before the finance approval stage. Also pass the required payload parameters.

17. Save and redeploy `LoanApplicationProcess` to involve the partner. Optionally, we can also call the notification service to e-mail or SMS the partner before sending in the task.

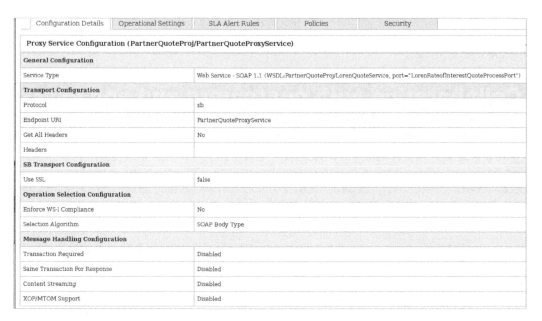

Configuration Details	Operational Settings	SLA Alert Rules	Policies	Security

Proxy Service Configuration (PartnerQuoteProj/PartnerQuoteProxyService)	
General Configuration	
Service Type	Web Service - SOAP 1.1 (WSDL:PartnerQuoteProj/LorenQuoteService, port="LorenRateofInterestQuoteProcessPort")
Transport Configuration	
Protocol	sb
Endpoint URI	PartnerQuoteProxyService
Get All Headers	No
Headers	
SB Transport Configuration	
Use SSL	false
Operation Selection Configuration	
Enforce WS-I Compliance	No
Selection Algorithm	SOAP Body Type
Message Handling Configuration	
Transaction Required	Disabled
Same Transaction For Response	Disabled
Content Streaming	Disabled
XOP/MTOM Support	Disabled

How it works...

Let's understand the output by considering our use case scenario:

1. Applicant James Cooper logs in to the James Bank Portal and submits his loan application online.

2. After a series of approvals—that is after document check, agency verification check, KYC check, and before finance approval—**Partner Quote Officer Irving Stone** gets this application request to quote a rate of interest that Loren Kelleher Bank can offer.

3. Loren Kelleher Bank offers a rate of interest that is less than the rate of interest quoted by James Bank to the loan applicant. Irving Stone quotes 6 percent for fixed and 8 percent for variable rate of interest to James Bank.

The output of this recipe is an integration scenario that showcases how the process integrates with the business partner's processes that are exposed over the OSB layer.

In reality, partners might take longer than expected to respond. In such a situation, it is always advisable to have a timeout default sequence (or a timer catch event) that waits for a specific period of time and then takes an alternative path. Once the timeout has occurred, it can send a reminder to the partner, or go ahead with the process without a partner quote, or ask for a quote from another partner.

There's more...

In many financial scenarios, partners can also communicate with each other using business-to-business (B2B) transactions over XML gateways. They can also exchange documents in prespecified formats.

Collaborating with customers and end users (Simple)

While writing this book, I interacted with several people who work at financial services at higher and senior management levels, to understand the challenges faced by them in the financial sector. One of the feedback received was that *competition* was getting tougher in the financial sector with private houses entering the banking and investment sector, and government allowing them to operate legally as long as they comply with the regulatory requirements.

The survival of these institutions depends on a very thin profit margin. With competition at its highest level, it gives them minimum scope to reject customers' request or deny customer satisfaction. They also need to be technically up-to-date to survive and meet customers' demands. There is no single technology, business process, or a single software application that can solve all the business requirements of an enterprise organization—be it a bank, an insurance company, or any other financial services. The solution architecture always comes with multiple technologies and applications working closely together. Some of the standard and reference architectures and prebuilt process packs help to a large extent, especially with respect to regulatory requirements, compliance, standard-based architecture, best practices, and ease of use.

Getting ready

Before we begin, make sure to download the source code from the previous recipe.

In this recipe, we will expose a lightweight, fast-to-load mobile user interface for our customers, as a web-based user interface can be very heavy and non-user friendly on mobile devices. We will also create a few backend tables to display changes in the rate of interest of both fixed and variable rates over a period of time. We will use these tables in creating business reports and analytics for our business analysts.

How to do it...

Let's perform the following steps:

1. From the JDeveloper let's open the `Loan EMI UI Fusion` ADF project that we created earlier in the *Implementing a home loan process recipe.*

2. Create a simple JSPX page that can render on mobile devices. Let's drag-and-drop the data controls on the page as **Trinidad components**, which are preferred lightweight components on mobile devices.

3. Deploy the process, access it over a mobile device or a mobile simulator, and test it.

4. Log in to WebCenter Portal and click on the **Administration** link.

5. Under the **Administration** tab, click on the **Resources** tab and in the **Mashup Styles**, select **Create Data Control**.

 These tables populate data pushed by one or more business processes.

6. Log in to WebCenter Content Server (`http://localhost:16200/cs`) and check in an HTML file that can be a public facing corporate page. Also, check in the related CSS and images files into a public folder, or a private folder, depending on the content security

How it works...

The output of this recipe is a customer facing portal that is also a part of a corporate intranet and extranet requirement, driven by the business process and business requirements.

Let us see how the whole setup of BPM, OSB, WebCenter Content, WebCenter Portal, BAM, and ADF Mobile work together from a financial services point of view.

1. James Cooper (loan applicant) checks the James Bank website on his mobile device to see if he has loan eligibility or not. Based on whether or not he does, the system generates a unique request ID that he can use later on for applying a loan.

 For more details, refer to the *How it works...* section of the *Implementing a home loan business process* recipe.

2. James Cooper visits the customer portal and sees the promotional campaign.

3. James Cooper applies for a home loan, as discussed in the *Integrating with business partners* recipe.

4. This action sends notification e-mails to Conan Doyle (Application Verification Officer) and John Steinbeck (Field Officer). They will verify the application and approve it to the next level.

5. The application is routed to the KYC check. An e-mail is sent back to James Cooper asking for KYC-related documents.

6. James Cooper logs in to the portal again, and submits the required KYC documents such as the Income Tax PAN, photograph, and passport copy.

7. The request is routed to Irving Stone (Partner Quote Officer) of Loren Kelleher Bank, and he sends a quote.

8. The quote is finally reviewed by William Faulkner (Finance Officer) of James Bank.

9. William Faulkner logs in on the WebCenter Portal's intranet and views some of the business dashboards that are related to changes in the rate of interest, the current status of various applications, corporate news, and any other task that needs his approval and decision making.

There's more...

BPM can be a great solution for financial services when viewed from the perspective of various roles, as discussed in the book. BPM with other Oracle Fusion Middleware technologies can help bring IT and the business closer together, increase customer satisfaction and corporate collaboration, and help to meet necessary regulatory requirements. It also helps to keep pace with changes in market trends and business dynamics, and to help adapt to new and emerging standards-based technologies and applications. As a next step, you might also want to have a look at ready-to-use **Oracle BPM Process Accelerators for financial services**.

Thank you for buying
Instant Oracle BPM for Financial Services How-to

About Packt Publishing

Packt, pronounced 'packed', published its first book *"Mastering phpMyAdmin for Effective MySQL Management"* in April 2004 and subsequently continued to specialize in publishing highly focused books on specific technologies and solutions.

Our books and publications share the experiences of your fellow IT professionals in adapting and customizing today's systems, applications, and frameworks. Our solution based books give you the knowledge and power to customize the software and technologies you're using to get the job done. Packt books are more specific and less general than the IT books you have seen in the past. Our unique business model allows us to bring you more focused information, giving you more of what you need to know, and less of what you don't.

Packt is a modern, yet unique publishing company, which focuses on producing quality, cutting-edge books for communities of developers, administrators, and newbies alike. For more information, please visit our website: www.packtpub.com.

Writing for Packt

We welcome all inquiries from people who are interested in authoring. Book proposals should be sent to author@packtpub.com. If your book idea is still at an early stage and you would like to discuss it first before writing a formal book proposal, contact us; one of our commissioning editors will get in touch with you.

We're not just looking for published authors; if you have strong technical skills but no writing experience, our experienced editors can help you develop a writing career, or simply get some additional reward for your expertise.

Oracle BPM Suite 11g: Advanced BPMN Topics

ISBN: 978-1-84968-756-0   Paperback: 114 pages

Master advanced BPMN for Oracle BPM Suite including inter-process communication, handling arrays, and exception management

1. Cover some of the most commonly misunderstood areas of BPMN

2. Gain the knowledge to write professional BPMN processes

3. A practical and concise tutorial packed with advanced topics which until now had received little or no documentation for BPM Suite developers and architects

---

Oracle BPM Suite 11g Developer's cookbook

ISBN: 978-1-84968-422-4   Paperback: 512 pages

Over 80 advanced recipes to develop rich, interactive business processes using the Oracle Business Process Management Suite

1. Full of illustrations, diagrams, and tips with clear step-by-step instructions and real time examples to develop Industry Sample BPM Process and BPM interaction with SOA Components

2. Dive into lessons on Fault ,Performance, and Rum Time Management

3. Explore User Interaction, Deployment, and Monitoring

Please check **www.PacktPub.com** for information on our titles

Made in the USA
Las Vegas, NV
18 January 2022